LIVING A REGRET.LESS LIFE

LITTLE THINGS THAT MATTER

SIDDHANT SHARMA

To everyone,

Who miss me when they feel low.

Love you Maa.

Miss you Boo.

Contents

Contents

Contents

LIVING A REGRET.LESS LIFE

It was a Saturday morning, I could still remember the sun rays bouncing on my face under that Eucalyptus tree. Teardrop ran down my cheeks making it hard for me to see clearly. All I could see was the clear blue sky, could hear the cicadas singing, could feel the chilly wind hitting against my chest as I sat under that tree. I used to sit there whenever I felt low. I was a thirteen-year-old kid who had no friends, insecure and missed his parents who lived in a different state. Life in a residential school was not as fun as I expected. I used to cry every day, complaining about how life isn't fair to me, about the people who weren't nice to me, made fun of me. I was all alone with my brother surviving every day as a soldier does in war, hoping everything would get better someday.

Time passed In a blink of an eye didn't even realise I was fifteen. Things didn't get better. I grew stronger, mentally. I realised over time that no one is gonna come save me, no one's gonna push me to be my best every day. The only best friend I had was myself. After going through a rough time at an early age, life taught me to be self-sufficient and many other life lessons that I have mentioned in this book.

There was a time when I no longer used to cry anymore. I smiled at every obstacle. Every problem seemed so tiny and worthless when I realised what happened, why it happened and why it won't happen anymore. Since then life has been beautiful, I don't fear disappointments, failures cause no matter what anyone says, it is a part of your life, everything happens for a reason. You learn from it, you evolve yourself over time, knowing what to do next every time you are in a mess. I learned how to tame my mind. What to let in and what not to. Because, deep down I knew back when I was thirteen, that this is not what I am, this isn't how my life should be, this isn't my purpose. I still have to experience and learn much more than what I already know.

I met wonderful people when I entered high school. If anyone of you are reading this, I would like to thank you for making every single day count. Those were some of the best phases, where I laughed with many, cried together, got punished together for not completing the assigned homework and made tons of memories. I am glad I met you all. Thank you for just existing and being there. Cheers to the Optimum Batch (It was where I prepared for JEE).

Special thanks to my homies who were there whenever I was in need. Making me feel like a part of their family, inviting me over for dinner and family gatherings. I love you all.

Life gets interesting when you are sure about yourself first. People and friends are just a part of the large world you are in yourself. Learn to love, forgive, and give yourself a second chance to yourself. Because you deserve it.

I wish you luck and strength to overcome your hard times, I hope you get over everything and live a life you always desired. Stay Safe and Keep Smiling.

Regards,
Siddhant Sharma.

৪৩

PREFACE

Dear Reader,

Thank you for choosing this book. This is the first time I have written my heart out in a form of a handbook. Inside is a compilation of true events and life lessons that I learned throughout my journey till now. And have tried my best to explain each one of them, separately.

I have come across many people dealing with hard times in their lives, they taught me many things in return to be heard and be understood. I would like to thank them to teach me things that would have taken decades to realise and experience. You have my respect for not giving up on yourself and fighting back.

This book is solely dedicated to people dealing with hardships in life who are confused and caught up in the same loop of disappointments, overthinking and pain. This handbook will show you light throughout the dark tunnel till you realise that the happiness and peace you seek is nowhere but, inside you.

I hope you discover the answers to your unanswered questions in life and learn to be the best version of yourself till the end by LIVING A REGRET.less LIFE.

Please do mail me to share your life experiences or a tale where you realte things mentioned in the book and let me know how did it influence you to look at life from a different perspective. I will try my best to respond to your emails and texts.

I wish you peace, strength and prosperity and tons of smiles throughout the journey. See you on the other side.

Siddhant Sharma

E-mail address – forsakenkid067@gmail.com

ACKNOWLEDGEMENTS

WRITING A BOOK IS MUCH TOUGHER THAN I THOUGHT AND MORE satisfying than I could have ever imagined. I feel so light. None of this would have been possible without my favourite people, Aiko and Hana. I met them when I was on a vacation In Jamshedpur. They stood by me during good times, because the bad things are invisible when we were together. We did have a few ups and downs, but this book is what it's all about.

I am eternally grateful for myself, to sacrifice my sleep for weeks when I had my academic submissions every week. Thanks to my parents who gave me *sanskaars* taught me to love, respect and so much more that's helping me in my journey to fulfilling my purpose in life. I truly have no idea where I'd be if I didn't have a tough childhood. I don't regret losing my childhood to what I am capable of today. I am glad that I did this. I always knew I could.

I

LIFE NEVER TREATS YOU FAIR, BUT IT'S NOT BAD EITHER.

How have you been?

I have been waiting for fifteen minutes standing at the entrance porch of the mall, and my dear friend, who promised to be on time is late as usual. He always had this habit of showing up late and cancelling plans at the last moment since our preparation for JEE Mains. It's been just two years knowing him but yet feels like a total stranger to me. Every meeting with him feels like a new experience with a stranger, yet close.

I met him when I was in 11th, we were in a coaching Institute preparing for Mains. He joined a week late. It was his first day, sitting all alone on the first bench where I used to sit, not that I was a bright student or interested in the lectures, but the faculty knew my father, so you know, formalities. I entered the classroom looking at the new student with his head buried in H.C Verma. That was the moment I knew I am going to deal with a studious student with high ambitions and a goal to achieve great success in life.

Playing Games, going on long drives with friends, attending uninvited marriages just to eat ice cream and Chinese food, flirting with the class ladies, talking all day about the movies was more of my game. I was a mess. And I thought he was just the opposite of what I am. But to my surprise, we were in the same boat. Although he was not into any outdoor sport or flirting with the senoritas, he was still one of the most interesting people I ever met.

Note: He was far better in academics and studies than I was.

Time passed in a blink of an eye and here we were preparing for our 12th Board. After all the fun we did back in 11th was paying back to us. You know Karma does hit hard. He scored far better grades than me. I was happy for all my buddies who scored more than me, I always believed in them, that they are going to do great things in their lives. As for me, I had barely passed my boards. And it was the turning point of our lives where we had to go our paths chasing our dreams and ambitions. It was a heart-breaking moment but goodbyes ended with smiles on our faces. And here we are now meeting him after two years of our goodbye.

It's been twenty minutes now, finally, the moron showed up, we shared a look smiling and moving towards each other. I was pleased to see him in a good shape. We shook hands and hugged sharing a friendly look, and asked him: **How have you been?** I could see his smile fade away, as he looked towards the ground.

Life has all types of surprises and presents for you, it's unpredictable. One day you may be as happy as a child who just got chocolate, and the next moment you can be the same child whose chocolate slipped in a ditch.

Life was fun back in 11th and 12th, felt like it was all life should bless me with, till the end. Endless chit-chats, countless dates, never-ending long drives, waiting for your crush to go home after she finished her tuition classes, trespassing prohibited areas just for the extra kick and whatnot. Those two years were the most memorable ones to date.

But now, things are different, you don't have friends from the most cherished part of your life, you don't meet each other daily, you barely contact each other now. It feels unfair as a teenager, why do things have to take a turn? It was all so jolly-molly back then. But it's the truth, change is inevitable, and with time it will bring even more surprises, good or bad depending upon the situation. One should not feel bad about it, after all, it's life, what else are you expecting? An ice-cream?

Give your life another chance. It's not fair but isn't bad either.

II

WHEN CONFUSED, FLIP A COIN.

When it comes to making decisions, this is the best hack I use. Now, you would be thinking, how can one decide life or death situations, or maybe a decision based on a serious relationship or any other decision where you are confused and don't know what to do, how to move forward in life, there's always this fear of making a wrong choice and regretting it later. One becomes so, unsure and under-confident that most of the time, they end up making the wrong choice.

The purpose of flipping a coin isn't to make decisions from its outcome but is to know what you want to choose when the coin is in mid-air. Assign the options to each face of the coin, flip it and when it's halfway up there, the very first option which you expect to come is the one, that you always wanted to go with, since the beginning, the only confusion was whether it's the right choice to make or not. Once, you realise what you want to do in a confused state, you have already got your answer. Even if you feel bad about abandoning the other choice, you have probably made the right choice for yourself. Some situations do need a more thoughtful and impartial choice, where one may regret it later in their life.

But to date, this little trick hasn't disappointed me. Not that I am always happy with the consequences, but in the end, I am satisfied that I chose what felt right, always trust your instincts in such situations because even if you were wrong you wouldn't blame someone else for the choice you made. Only you would be responsible for the decision you made, no matter what the choice was.

It's always better to choose than to be confused throughout the phase. After all, one day you will have to choose any one of them. Then why create pressure, overthink and be a pain to people, while you can just flip a coin and be satisfied with making a choice!

III
CONTROL YOUR ANGER.

"Speak when you are angry and you'll make the best speech you'll ever regret".

-Harriet Ward Beecher

When there's a clash between what you expect and what you receive your brain's circuit sounds an alarm. Activity is triggered in a small region in the brain called the Amygdala, which processes emotions of anger, fear and anxiety. Fear and anger generate a common stress response of **Flight** or **Fight.**

The fear makes us want to flee the situation whereas anger sparks up the urge to fight back. In the end, either of them is not healthy for a mentally stable person. Anger is well known for destroying relationships. It is one of the common feelings that a person feels, it may range from a mild annoyance to profound rage. Anger creates an aura around itself which not only affects one's mental state but their behaviour around people too. Till now, you must have realised what will the anger cost you. Not to mention health problems and psychological issues caused by it.

So, what should one do?

Tips to manage anger :

- Always remember, that it's you who is responsible for the state of your mind, and no one else.
- Anger should not be expressed instantly, give yourself time to process the rage.
- When the anger triggers, keep your voice down.
- Recognize the cause of anger.
- Ask yourself, is the anger helping you feel better.
- Look at the situation from their's shoes.
- Agree to Disagree.
- Avoid predicting what they must be thinking.
- Control the situation with Kindness.

Techniques to manage anger :

- Express your feelings to a person, you trust.
- Maintain a diary: Write down things that trigger your anger.
- Let the other person know that you are angry with them.
- Analyse the benefits and loss of being angry.
- Develop an empathetic nature towards the person, you are angry with. It'll help you analyse the situation from a second perspective.

When handled properly, anger can serve as a positive force that can motivate people to make changes. However, it is important to recognize when it is excessive and harmful. Doing so can help you reduce the harm caused by your anger.

IV

NOBODY THINKS OF YOU, DON'T OVERTHINK.

"Overthinking is no big deal when you know when to let go"

-Siddhant Sharma

No matter what others say, the truth is nobody knows you better than you. We are caught up in a loop of overthinking things that might not even be important to others. Sometimes, lack of confidence and fear of being judged makes us doubt our existence in that situation. We are stuck up in how we look and sound to others when there's hardly a chance that they might be thinking about us.

Let's just look at an example:

We're constantly scrolling through hundreds of videos and photos on social media platforms, every day without pausing to think about the artist. Remember the last time you looked at someone's Instagram post to notice how they're posing for a photo? Or how many takes did it take to create the final content or how many people were involved in the act or what would they all have done after shooing the video and whatnot.

You can go all day thinking about new kinds of stuff and creating imaginations that barely have any importance. Let's say, even if you think about something or someone specific, how long does the memory last, or how long does it bother you or make you feel things. Falling in love at the first sight is an exception here, Haha Just kidding.

Don't let your own opinion stop you from doing things that you like, people usually step back and drop down the idea of doing their favourite activities just because they overthink people overthinking about them. Just let it go, you only live once, why sacrifice the precious moments just for the sake of something, that doesn't matter. Do give it a thought.

V

PAY BACK YOUR LOANS ON TIME.

One would never understand the situation until they are the one lending out money to others. Let's imagine a situation where instead of being the one in debt, you are the good person, helping out your friend.

"A friend approaches you and asks if he can borrow the money from you. He agrees to pay by the end of next month. You, as a good friend, rented him some money to help him with his financial problems.

That's a month ago, and your friend now avoids you. Whenever you approach him about his loan, he will find a reason for not having the money and will promise to pay you back very soon. This cycle may last several months. As a result, the friendship gets complicated and feelings are hurt. What was once a wonderful relationship, now has become an emotional burden.

Every month that the loan is not paid, you lose hope of ever receiving your money back. As a result, you become consumed by rage and frustration towards your friend."

Can you relate?

How would you make your friend start repaying what he owes if you were this person?

Have you ever had to break a bond with a person because of money?

How did you deal with it?

Everyone experiences this at least once in their life from a family member or a friend. The reasons may vary, but almost always we want to be a good friend, which leads us to lend a helping hand.

"Neither a borrower nor a lender be."

It is a famous Shakespeare line from Hamlet. Although, I disagree with the belief. But, it does raise an interesting point. Doesn't it?

You cannot buy trust or relationships with money, my friend. If borrowed, payback on time, don't do something which you'll feel guilty about, your entire life.

VI
SACRIFICE FOR YOUR LOVED ONES.

I am not married, nor do I have children, but when I become a father I would do anything and everything to protect them, make them happy, and give them the best childhood they could have. I am sure, any parent would do the same. One morning I was going through the newspaper and came across a short story. It was probably the most touching story I ever read. I couldn't remember the exact plot, but I'll try my best to narrate it to you.

So, here it goes –

One fine day, Shikha an 8-year-old girl asked her dad," What will you gift me for my 12th Birthday?"

He replied," It's going to be a surprise!."

When Shikha turned 11 years old, she fainted and was taken to hospital. The doctor told her father that her heart is weak and she will probably die in a few months.

Her dad went to see her, while she was lying on the hospital bed, she whispered, "papa…did they tell you I am going to die? " Her father replied; "no dear, you are going to live" as he was about to leave the ward.

Shikha held his hand and asked," You think so?" He turned around weeping and said," I know so, princess."

After a few months, she turned 12. She was soon released from the hospital and was recovering, she came home to discover a letter on her bed which said…." My honeybee, if you are reading it now, that means everything went well, just as I promised you that day. Do you remember the day when you asked me what I was going to gift you on your 12th birthday? I didn't know what to say then, but my gift to you was MY HEART."

He Had Donated His Heart!

"There's nothing greater than a man laying down his life for his loved ones".

Have you ever sacrificed something for someone in your life?

or

Did someone sacrifice for you?

In life, there are circumstances where sacrifices have to be made, not just for someone, but sometimes for your sake too. It doesn't matter if the sacrifice made was for good or bad. If done for your loved ones without them knowing about it is the biggest gift they can ever receive from you.

Don't hesitate to make them happy, even if it takes some of your happiness. Life's too short to be selfish for favourite ones.

VII

BE THERE FOR SOMEONE WHEN THEY ARE IN NEED.

Break yourself down to pieces and give them away, Fill in the voids with the pieces of your cherished ones. Be there for someone, by investing in them. Take good care, because they are important and a part of you too because you feel what they feel.

Not just hear, but listen to them. Become familiar with how they speak, how they feel, how they express themselves. Observe their body language, the slight change in their tone, their ticks. Master the art of listening till you know it's the time to absorb. Decide, when to be an acoustical sounding panel, and when to think like a child, taking every single detail in your mind quietly.

Being there for someone means giving it all at the moment. Make yourself quiet, small and present in the moment.

When apart, imagine the situation from their end. Try to read the silence, the meaning behind those empty lines. Keep a good understanding of the emojis they usually use to express themselves. Understand their situation by observing the time taken to read and reply to your texts. Pick up their call, when you know they want someone to talk to, and sometimes just call them, because you missed them. They won't feel bad.

Give them surprise treats, Make them tea when they have a sore throat. Learn to spot what they desire but would not ask for, and things they need but are unaware of.

Embrace them at their best, embrace them at their lowest. Tickle them, like you used to do it back in assembly when you were in third grade, lock your legs while watching T.V with them. Remind them that they are important to you, keep the physical touch alive.

Protect them, but not too much, Don't let your feelings for them be a burden to their problems. Let them try to take a stand for themselves. Give them space to grow, to get strong. Don't let go, when they are in need. Learn to understand when they need personal space and when they ask for it because both are not the same. Be like an environment for them where they can feel safe to be sad, happy, angry, crazy and vulnerable. But be aware not to get driven away by their emotion.

Understand that often being there for others involves sacrificing your priorities. Realize that while this isn't always healthy or good, it is sometimes needed. Know that sometimes the person you need to be there for is yourself and that you will be able to give different amounts at different times in your life. Being there for someone else is more about being mentally engaged and emotionally available for someone other than yourself than it is about being physically present.

Try doing it for someone, and you'll add an achievement to your life. Achievement of happiness.

VIII

START SAVING MONEY, JUST FOR YOURSELF.

Can money buy happiness? What do you say, reader?

You must have heard this question quite a lot of times in your life. Well, even before answering that, have we questioned ourselves even once, What is money and Why is it so necessary in everyone's life?

We have five senses known as taste, smell, touch, hearing, and sight. I have assumed money as the sixth sense which has the power and capacity to satisfy all the fives senses mentioned above. Where there is money, there is power. And hence, money is a valuable liquid asset in one's life. Since childhood, we have been taught by our parents to use money wisely, even if it's a school trip, an outing with friends or a town fair. But we as naughty kids wanted to explore every single thing that caught out little eyes and made our hearts skip a beat. My twenties made me realise things that I shouldn't have wasted my money on and things that hold a much greater value than any other things I bought.

Do you know what is the best thing to invest your money on?

Money is an asset and assets are supposed to be used thoughtfully. The best thing to invest in is YOURSELF.

Here, investing in yourself doesn't mean, buying fancy clothes, hanging out in clubs, eating at expensive restaurants or requesting your dad to buy a sports bike because you have scored good marks in your exam. For the time being, all these things may sound and feel good to experience. But sooner or later, these things are going to be a liability to you and liabilities can never provide you with money, whereas they are the ones that reduce your savings.

Invest in learning. Acquire multiple skills that will help you survive even in the hardest of situations. Gain knowledge, so that when you go through a bad time in the future, you can utilize the knowledge and work to buy yourself bread and butter.

So, why saving is so important?

- Saving lets you eventually buy things you might not have enough money for right now.
- It can keep you out of a debt in an emergency.
- Saving means self-reliance.
- Saving provides more financial freedom in the future.
- Saving helps you shape the possible.

Everyone should learn how to save. It allows you to buy things that might otherwise be beyond of reach, keeps you out of debt, and increases your independence. It usually means you can do more since you have more options or have more money. As a result, you will be happier. Saving, above all, encourages you to keep your eyes on your goals. Make a plan. Take a look forward. You may achieve your goals by saving!

• 19 •

IX

EAT ICE CREAM, IF YOU WANT TO REMEMBER THAT MOMENT.

Have you ever felt nostalgic passing a lane, and you smell something familiar but are unable to recall the moment you smelled that last time? There's a faint memory running in a loop in your mind about the moment that you wanna recall but you're not able to?

Well, this is because the human mind tends to connect every special moment they want to remember with the five senses, may it be touch, hearing, smell, taste or sight.

More than 12 million smell receptors are located throughout the nose and nasal cavity in the human olfactory system. These receptors collect odour molecules from the air and send electrical impulses to the olfactory bulb, a small structure in the brain that processes them.

And hence, the role of taste in flavour is why food has such a high potential for evoking memories.

Icecreams have always been one of my favourite desserts when it comes to making a moment memorable. Although I don't eat ice cream often, I remember those moments when I did eat it, because it has this invisible connection, relating the moments to the senses.

It all started back when I was in 11th grade, I and my friend had a bucket list for ourselves where we had decided to try out every flavour of the ice cream that one of the parlours used to sell. So, one day after our school we went to the parlour as usual to try a new flavour, I still remember I had chosen a choco-chip bar, and he had the mango flavour. We sat outside the parlour discussing the homework given to us for the next day. We were caught up in ourselves until a girl of our age came out of the shop, her face was covered up with a stole and I couldn't see her face, though she seemed beautiful. Meanwhile, this friend of mine was also looking at her at the same time. You know, men will be men.

So she came out of the parlour and was about to leave the scene on her ride, but she stopped and realised that we were looking at her with an exceptional amount of interest that lead us to share a moment just looking at each other in the eyes. My heart skipped a beat, I am sure he felt it too. It was all so sudden, we were very simple guys, busy with our movies, games and other fantasy stuff. But this was at a different level for us. I was surprised to look at a girl in her eyes for more than five seconds. That was an achievement for both of us. The moment was broken by the honking of a school bus, as she was leaving, she laughed looking at us making it the loudest goodbye.

And since then, every time I eat ice cream, I tend to remember that moment. Well, of course, the object can change from person to person but who doesn't like ice cream? J

X

LET GO OF THE PAST, WHAT'S GONE IS GONE.

Do you usually feel lost as you move into the future? The past may probably be the best place to stay. It's a place you're familiar with; a place where you can engage with it.

You've already had your fill of it. And, no matter how bad it was, it's not in doubt. The future appears to be a dark hole into which you are being thrown. There could be cushions or cement at the bottom – you never know. Worse, there may be more despair and falling – maybe forever.

However, it is inevitable. Fate will always be ahead of you, and you will always be moving in that direction. So, the best move for you is to let go of your emotional connection to the past. The past is no longer present – it exists only in your memory.

You can no longer live in the past. You may have liked it and grown fond of it. You've become so attached to it that you're having second thoughts about letting it go. But, no matter how much you wish for it, it will never return. You must do the difficult thing here – let that go.

True, it will take some time. You'll need to be patient. Try to get it out – try to just get ahead. You will be able to do so eventually. You can always find solace in the past. Of course, moments can be used to comfort yourself, to make you proud of a moment when you achieved something great. But don't get too caught up in it. Learn from the mistakes, and walk away. The past can never be our present, it has to change.

Accept that life must go on. Embrace that the past has passed and that the present has taken its place. The present will also vanish, and the only way you will be heading towards will be the future. It's inevitable. To get to the future, all you have to do is gather the confidence of your previous lessons and move forward.

Be thankful for the present moment. Be thankful for what you already have. Particularly the simple things. We are always aspiring for such big goals that we forget to be thankful for the little things, such as a cool breeze on a warm summer day or the first drop of rain. Be inspired in yourself, and then start inspiring others.

There are so many opportunities in the future, so it is not always gloomy. All you have to do is look at it through your eyes. Be optimistic about the future. Know that it is there to help you shape yourself – to help you become who you are.

You must trust that you can accept the future and use it to better yourself. It's not easy – but defining oneself has never been easy. Believe in the dreams you've created. Even if you are unsure what you want to do, believe that you will figure a way out. Be ready for it!

XI

DON'T FORGET TO CRY, IT DOESN'T MAKE YOU WEAK.

"Crying is not only a human reaction to sorrow and distress, but it's also a healthy one," says neurobiologist and tear researcher Dr William H. Frey II, PhD. Crying is a natural way to relieve emotional stress, which, if not addressed, has direct negative effects on the body, including increased cardiovascular risk and other stress-related disorders."

According to studies, 85% of women and 73% of men feel less angry and depressed after crying than they did earlier. Many people believe that crying makes them soft and incapable of dealing with their hearts and emotions, when in fact, crying does the exact opposite!

Although anybody can cry, not everyone is capable of doing so. People who cry are thought to be weak, according to a self-defeating belief system. We make fun of people who cry publicly and take pride in the fact that we don't reveal our feelings. Isn't it strength to cry to meet society's expectations of strength?

To prove that you are human, it takes guts to exhibit your weakness to others, to indicate that you are doubtful, cheated, dissatisfied, etc. Even more, courage is required to recognise to oneself that we have been tricked and shamed, that we all can control every single thing that comes into our lives, and we are not as strong as we thought we were.

Crying allows us to release all of the negativity we've been holding inside. It's almost like a little tradition that marks the end of a terrifying experience. We generally cry when we feel we have no other choice - there is no convincing the other, no hoping the other to change, no going to wait for things to get better, no trying to remove the pain someone has caused us. After we've cried, accepted that some memories were terrible, and accepted that what happened was extremely painful, we can move on to the next episode of our lives.

Individuals who do not cry, even if they want to, do not provide themselves with the necessary closure. Their pain remains bottled up inside, and you already know what happens when emotions go unspoken: they find their way into our daily conversations and are likely to explode one day into unrelated things. This is a weakness because all of our negativity increases the likelihood that we will impact ourselves and others in the long run. A strong person can move forward with no baggage from the past.

So let us stop deceiving ourselves and others into thinking we don't feel pain. I don't understand why people take pride in demonstrating that they are made of concrete when God gave them such a lovely ability to experience. This is a mysterious world we live in!

XII

BE CONSISTENT, TRUST THE PROCESS.

"It's not an act for once, but a habit forever"

-Siddhant Sharma

Life can be tough. Sailing the ocean will bring you troubled water, just as your life journey will bring you challenging times. It is a fact that everyone has experienced at some time in their lives while trying to attain a goal or maintain a degree of consistency. This is true for startups, fitness, and other determined lifestyle choices.

What's the purpose of your life?

Till we get to the consistency aspect, let's look at what life is all about. Make a list of your objectives and write them down.

Is it for the goal of building a small business? Going to the gym daily? Improving your creative skills? Or should you simply be a better person? Make a visual image of what you will feel if you achieve all of your goals. Consider your life at that point.

Now, put down the pen and consider the following critical question: What is the purpose of your life?

We only have a small period on Earth, so making the most of it and sharing our joys is essential. To achieve this, we must have a reason to get out of bed every morning, with a smile on our face, eagerly awaiting the new day. That's where your goals list comes into play. People are always excited when they feel progress in their lives, such as when they move to a new location, get a new job, travel, lose weight, or gain more business. Goals will help you feel this way, as well as happier and more energetic.

To achieve these objectives, you must be emotionally invested in them. It has to be your hopes and dreams! That is why you must create a visual picture of how it will feel to reach them. Your emotions have a large influence on your choices, and you should use them proactively. When you are emotionally invested in your goals, you will not only work to achieve them, but you'll also feel a lot better and more alive along the way.

Having meaningful goals gives meaning to your life. Your life will have a goal, no matter how simple it is. Every day that you make progress toward that goal will feel like a good day.

This is where consistency comes into the picture.

Being Consistent.

Consistency is the difference between failures and successes. If you are unable to maintain a consistent level of an attempt to achieve the goal, you will most likely return to your old habits and simply give up. Worse, you'll have the impression that you're not living up to your principles or achieving your life's purpose. You can drown out this emotion with TV, snacks, or other vibes, but the sense of failure will remain deep within you.

You must be consistent in your choices and in the goal you have chosen. Make a promise to yourself.

Once you promise yourself that you could achieve this goal, it is time to reveal a fantastic tool that will help you. Just keep in mind that the push has to come from you. No one else will be able to help you. Remember that consistency does not imply giving your all every time. It is about remaining firm. You keep going despite the lows and also the highs. It all gets down to maintaining a steady push toward your goal.

XIII

KEEP THE RELATIONSHIP PRIVATE, UNTIL IT'S PERMANENT.

Everyone is unique. I know people who only have one social media profile for themselves as a couple (I could never be that but for them, it works). Friends of mine post about their relationships on social media daily, and it works for them. I enjoy seeing updates and seeing couples I care about enjoying life and one another. Trying to keep your relationship secret is a personal choice and should be mutually decided. But, regardless of what you or your partner share or do not share, the only thing important is that you both truly value each other more than other people's opinions.

Displaying your relationship is similar to seasoning a dish with salt. You can still add more, but once you've shared private information and made your relationship public, it's impossible to undo. You may be sorry for oversharing and allowing others into the insides of your relationship, but you'll never be sorry for keeping your peace. Realize, you can always season with salt. And, when used judiciously, salt is far more effective.

I've had many friends dealing with relationship issues. Everywhere, I've been too, always met a guy or two, seeking advice on their relationship. And neither of them ever have regretted maintaining their relationship a secret.

Less is More. Of course, things just happen and we talk to our friends, but one should always do so with their partner's best interests in mind. We are ignited and want to tell everyone about it. We need them to tell us that we're not insane and that our partner was mistaken (but still loves us).

Even if you tell every detail to your friends, no one knows exactly what happens behind closed doors. When you run to your relatives and friends every time there's a problem, it's a tricky and unhealthy slope. Disagreements and arguments are easily forgotten, but not so for the people who gave it all to be there with you.

All in a nutshell:

It's hard to find and maintain a healthy relationship in today's world of constant distractions. So, why invite much more drama and confusion? Particularly if you are the one who has control over the door.

When you keep your relationship personal, you shut off to the superficial and open up to the kinds of significant benefits that can only flourish between two people.

Your relationship is your business and no one else's. Maintain some mystery. Keep your cool and stay on the safer side.

If there's one thing I've learned as a teenager growing up is that :

The fewer others know, the more you grow.

XIV
LIFE IS TOO SHORT TO WHINE ABOUT LOSSES.

"The time taken to regret a loss is still a loss"

-Siddhant Sharma

Everyone goes through the traumatic experience in their unique way and has different ways to deal with grief. While a loss is one of the most painful experiences a person can have in their lifetime, it can also teach them how to live their lives in a more interactive and rewarding way. Pain can teach those who are experiencing it, many valuable lessons and allow them to develop a deeper love of life.

Strengthen the bond.

Grieving is one of the most isolating experiences you will ever have. Because grieving is such an individualistic process, everyone goes through it differently and in various lengths of time. Some people walk away when they are troubled, but they are unlikely to be the only ones affected by the loss.

Reaching out to others who are going through a hard time can help in making the process more bearable. You will also notice that your connections with those who are assisting you or who are grieving would become much better and stronger. Even if a person's death only has a direct effect on you, there are sources of support for those dealing with a loss that can help them manage their emotions.

Be grateful for what you already have.

A loss will make you rethink that nothing lasts forever and that we must be grateful for what we already have in the present moment. A loss, whether traumatic or expected, will make you appreciate the happiness and real relationships in your life with a newfound appreciation. As your gratefulness grows, so will your relationships, and then you will find more satisfaction in the small details.

Live like it's your last day on earth.

As cheesy as it sounds, you should live every day as if it were your last. Loss and sadness are difficult to deal with, but they can teach you how to live your life to the fullest. Because tomorrow isn't guaranteed, make the most of today and take delight in the limited, beautiful opportunities that life has to offer.

XV

DON'T BE RUDE, YOU NEVER KNOW WHAT THE OTHER PERSON IS GOING THROUGH.

I was in fifth grade at the time. One of my best friends was competing in a fancy dress competition. My friends were everything to me back then. I would go against everyone to fight for them.

She was going to play the role of Radha, but she had this large pimple on her nose. The performance was scheduled for the following day. So, way back home on the school bus, one of the girls made fun of her appearance as Radha with a big pimple on her nose.

I was offended, and being possessive about her uttered the below:

"How would you feel if someone told you that one of your legs is shorter than the other?"

I didn't realise I was making fun of a physically challenged girl until I said these words. I made an apology as soon as we got off the bus. (We lived next door). It's been 15 years since this incident, but I'm still embarrassed by what I said that day. This is the most impolite thing I've ever done to someone, and I still feel bad for it to this day.

Though she has forgiven me, and we are good friends, I have not forgotten that incident.

We never know what's going on in someone's life—what news they got that day, maybe they just lost all their money or have a sick loved one. That is why it is important to lead with gentleness as often as possible.

Rather than taking things they say or do personally, give them the benefit of the doubt. I'm sure there were times when my reaction to small issues was out of proportion to what had been going on. I was doing my best to be nice and respectful and keep it together at the time. When I'm frustrated or annoyed by someone's actions, I alert myself that I don't know what's going on in with there life. I try to relax, not take it personally, and believe that they are doing their best.

You never know how a small gesture of kindness can make a difference in someone's life.

XVI

WRITE YOUR THOUGHTS TODAY, LAUGH AT THEM LATER.

I've been writing a diary since I was twelve years old. Yes. Since my seventh grade, I've kept a personal diary.

I still remember I was away from home in a residential school in Kodaikanal. Every day wasn't a good day, I had to go through many problems in a day with friends, teachers and daily needs. Not to mention, homesickness.

I'm was an introvert who found it difficult to convey my thoughts to others, so I decided to write them down in a diary along with the date and the respective day. It is the best thing I've ever done for myself because it contains every old memory, thought, feeling, experience, and other problem I've gone through as a child, teenager, and now as a 23-year-old.

Moreover, it contained facts, poems and short stories which I used to read in the library as a kid. And the last page was usually filled with my bucket list which is still in process.

I can see myself evolve throughout the time whenever I open it now. I could see how my character has changed over time. I notice how some things affected me as a child and how certain things no longer matter to me. It also astonishes me that I start to wonder, **"Was it me who wrote it?"** It's almost like doing a reality check to see where I've changed and where I've remained the same.

It also helps me get back to my natural self when I'm down because I remember how lively I was as a child to make my wishes come true. It's something that allows me to be positive and never lose focus of my true self.

With a throwback to my childhood whenever I have to recall. I don't have to ask my parents, sibling, or relatives how I was as a child. Everything is captured in that one thing. Turning those pages, that writing style, those dumb childhood philosophies of friendship and betrayal make me chuckle and, at times, tear up. That's something truly beautiful, and I always appreciate myself for having the sense to do so at the tender age of twelve.

Every person who keeps a diary can admit to just how incredible it is to read and go through your past all over again!

XVII

IT'S NEVER TOO LATE TO SAY SORRY OR THANK YOU.

Have you been in a position where a close friend or colleague does a favour for you and you don't thank them because you're used to it? Or in a position where you did or said things hurtful to a friend and didn't apologise right away because, once again, you're used to them? I believe the majority of us have.

I've grown "familiarised to them." What I mean is that we already realise how our friends are; we know their personality and attitude toward others, whether they are pleasant, cute, rude, egoistic, or whatever. So if your buddy has always been nice to you, it can get to the point where you don't think saying thank you is necessary (it is), and when they do something nice for you, something they don't usually do, something you think is worth more than a thank you, you don't say it. And, if you're like me, you begin to think about that later, "Oh, I should have wanted to thank them after that, why didn't I?" and the time passes. Saying sorry is the same way, and it bothers me most of the time. I have a feeling of guilt, and although I believe it is too late to apologise or thank, the guilt never truly goes away.

Sure, you could argue that the other party doesn't care, so it doesn't matter. However, it's more about feeling better in your heart and with yourself, and it isn't always about them. There's a reason they're known as the "Three magic words": Sorry, Please and Thank you. It has an impact on both the receiver's and the giver's emotions. When you thank someone, they feel valued. They believe they are making a positive difference in your life; I know I do when I am thanked, and I'm sure others do as well. Even if they appear to be uninterested in your gratitude or apologies, they have no idea how much it can warm their heart until they receive it. As for you, the provider, it's liberating, and it feels so good to make other people happy, since most of the time when you thank someone, you're greeted with a smile and the words "You're Welcome." I'm not sure about others, but I live for that smile; it's a wonderful feeling to simply let others know that they are valued.

So, if you're going to argue whether you should still say thank you or apologise, JUST DO IT ALREADY! Even if it's been two years, they may have forgotten; tell them, not in a harsh way, if you're going to apologise.

Remember that it also helps in the healing of your heart. Nobody deserves to be overwhelmed by the burden of guilt. If it's difficult, consider how much lighter you'd feel if you would just do it, and don't assume you have to say many words. Because they have already forgiven and most likely forgotten.

XVIII

FIGHT BACK FOR YOURSELF.

Life gives us multiple chances to fight back. Fight for your dignity, self-esteem, prestige, pride, motto, and identity. In today's world, it is very easy for anyone around us to shatter anything related to our soul. It could be a rejection of our existence or our ideas. People are filled with intense envy all around us.

We all have life goals that we all want to achieve, goals that will help us progress. The objectives that are most important to us are to make the future beautiful. The objectives will assist us in developing the identity that we have always desired. The goals are the very foundations of the professionalism we learn in our daily lives. The objectives that make us feel good about pursuing something.

Our objectives set us apart from the rest of the world. Our lives are so complicated that we don't stick to one goal and instead change them based on the circumstances we face. We don't have to change our goals just because we're having a bad day. To save the goals, we must fight the problems of daily life. The goals are similar to our identities in that they do not need to change every day. Fighting back against problems, strange situations, and people to save the goal is reasonable. We must maintain a high level of spirit not just in sports, but also in our daily lives.

Determine your life's passion and fight with everything you have to save it. It could be drawing, photography, music, theatre, or any other form of art or anything on the world's canvas. Fight back to keep it in you. When you feel as if you have nothing left in you, just engage yourself in your hobby. Time will fly by, and you will be completely oblivious to the boredom and rejection. It's all about attempting to fight back in life, fighting to keep your passion alive. Fighting to keep your hobbies alive in your heart. We must hold and fight to keep our hobby, just like a kid who refuses to give up a toy.

As we progress in life, some people become essential parts of our journey. Whatever circumstance we are in, those who always come to our rescue and prevent us from breaking. Do not allow them to leave. Start fighting back as many times as you need to, but don't let them out of your life. Relationships are important in our lives, just like any other aspect of our personality.

Who we are is defined by the people we spend time with. There'll be people who attach and leave according to their convenience, but those who connect and leave according to your concerns are crucial. Never let them go because they are gods in your life. Continue to fight for the survival of your primal instincts.

Fight back for yourself, not for anyone else. To save the truth in you, the human in you, the greed in you, the attitude in you, the habit in you, the love in you, and every other trait that characterises you as a human.

XIX

TOMORROW STARTS TODAY.

Whenever it comes to completing a task, get started as soon as possible. So why do you put it off until tomorrow if you have to do it? Start doing it right now!

"Don't postpone what you can do today until tomorrow."

The above-mentioned sentence was said by Sir Benjamin Franklin. Consider it for a moment. We can get a sense of his lifestyle from this sentence. He never put off work for the next day, even if there was time. And the result is right in front of us.

To achieve your goals begin today, not tomorrow. If you believe that the world will change soon, you are living in a fool's paradise. Tomorrow's world could be even worse than today's. So go ahead and do it right now. Today is the day to do it. Begin to move. Don't sit around silently. Famous author Julien Smith once said,

"There's not a single thing in life that is done better by starting tomorrow."

Can you recall anything you put off until the next day then completed? No, I don't believe so. I've kept off work several times in my life, and what I've discovered is that the promised tomorrow never arrives. Let me give you an illustration. My mother once told me that I needed to clean out my cupboard. It was during a vacation period. So I explained that I had a lot of chances. I'll do it the next day. My tomorrow, on the other hand, never came. My vacation had come to an end. My cupboard, on the other hand, remained a mess. It would be done if I cleaned my closet on the day my mother requested.

Just remember that you must act now or you will regret it later. If you postpone your tasks until the next day, you would never be able to complete them. As a result, you'll never achieve your desired success.

XX

BELIEVE IN MIRACLES, THERE'S NO END TO IT.

I don't seem to attract miracles because I'm "lucky". Since I believe in miracles, I attract them.

You see, without BELIEF, there is nothing. Because if you don't believe something is possible, your mind would never allow you to put forth the effort necessary to make it happen. Then, of course, you will strengthen your lack of faith by saying something like, "See... I knew it since the beginning, it wasn't going to happen." And when you Realize something will not happen, you are always right.

You don't have to believe me. Carry out your research. There is plenty of scientific evidence that indicates that your Beliefs create one's reality. The PLACEBO effect provides more than enough information to prove that your thoughts create your nature of reality. Because your beliefs are energy vibrations, if you want to entice positive vibes and optimistic people into your life, you must THINK and BELIEVE in them.

This will be difficult if you have a history of negativity and negative thinking. You will need to reprogram your mind to think more positively. It will take time, just as it took you time to taint your view on the world with negative energy. However, with practice, you can begin THINKING and ATTRACTING good into your life. You can begin BELIEVING in miracles and making them a part of your LIFE. You can RETURN TO FEELING decent ABOUT YOUR LIFE. You've earned it. You have earned the right to FEEL GOOD AGAIN.

You deserve to begin experiencing amazing relationships and beautiful friendships, and you deserve to discover and LIVE a deep, meaningful existence. This is not a naive assumption. This isn't just possible, but also necessary. Your THOUGHTS give rise to your REALITY. Begin to think BIGGER, BRIGHTER, and LIGHTER thoughts. Your THOUGHTS can either make you ill or make you well. Make an informed decision. Just see the bright side of every situation. Choose to Look at the positives in the world and spend time with people who SPEAK ABOUT IT and SEE IT.

YOU MAKE THE DECISION. You truly do. Not because of the circumstances. Not the difficulties. However, your reactions. You have complete control over those. REACT as if every emotion has an impact on your LIFE because it does. As a result, influence it with POSITIVITY. Choose to let miracles happen, Believe in them.

XXI

WRITE LOVE LETTERS TO YOUR FAVOURITE PERSON.

To most of us usual admirers, composing a love note would seem something from Shakespeare or another world we're unfamiliar with. After all, in today's world, we don't write a letter very often. So you're wondering why you'd want to write a love note to your favourite person. This is our logical aspect meddling once more.

Romance defies logic. It does, however, have its logic system. The love letter, like the date night, the anniversary, and many other things we do to make our loved ones happy, is not done for practical reasons. It makes them feel affectionate toward you, which leads to more love, more heartfelt romance, and much more exciting and fun dates if you spend some time together.

You don't always make a connection between a card, letter, or flowers and a later passionate moment. This is because men are very quick to think and react. Anything which takes place in the afternoon has no bearing on how compassionate we are with our lady that night. But, as you may already know, ladies are wired differently than men.

They will remember a romantic gesture made by you for hours. One grand gesture from you, such as flowers or a love letter, can evoke continued feelings of love in them for months or years to come. That is a fantastic investment. You get endless hours of devotion, affection, and genuine love from them for the little time you spent in learning how this makes their soul warm and shining with love for you, a wellspring of love that never goes dry.

There are numerous ways to use love letters to amplify your romance with your favourite person in your life.

- When separated, whether for a few weeks or an extended period. Writing a letter expressing your emotions for them becomes a cherished memory and small gift for themselves for the rest of their life.

- For special occasions such as anniversaries and birthdays. If you have sent them a love letter through the mail that day and they aren't expecting it, the surprise will spring up into a volcano of love in them. They will be delighted about your letter and surprise, and it will only cost you a few papers, a stamp, and possibly some minutes writing the letter.

So, how do you go about putting this amazing romantic tool to work for you? To compose them a love note that touches their heart, you don't have to be a novelist or a great writer. Follow these simple instructions:

- As you speak, write. Don't try to become "Mr/Ms Poetry" overnight. Just say what's on your mind, as if you were in the same room. It will be like a song to them when they "listen" to your voice in the letter.

- Allow private puns and shared memorable moments a point of discussion. "One of my favourite memories of our relationship is "the night we first hugged." They'll remember that moment fondly, and it'll make them smile. Furthermore, it will revive the romantic feelings they had towards you that night, making it feel new and exciting all over again.

- Avoid being dirty or graphic. It's natural for romance to lead to sex, but you don't have to force it. Don't talk about how much you "wish" for them sexually. Discuss feelings, emotions, romantic thoughts, and locations. Talk about hugging, kissing, and snuggling if you want to speak about intimacies. Those are the real deal, believe it or not.

The most important aspect of writing a love letter is to try it. Don't just ponder it; get a paper and pen and write one right now. Alternatively, get a card and perform on one. Don't give it too much thought. If you spend too much time thinking about what you're going to say or how you're going to do something, you'll become nervous and stop. Being spontaneous and just charging ahead is a great way to build a romantic letter that will touch them. Sure, you'll make mistakes, but the fact that you chose to act out of love and spontaneity for them will more than makeup for any typos or clumsy prose.

XXII

MAKE YOUR BRAIN, YOUR BEST FRIEND.

The mind has long been blamed and criticized as the source of all our troubles and problems. Because it drifts aimlessly and jumps from topic to topic, it's often referred to as 'Monkey Mind.' It jumps to conclusions and judgments without taking the time to understand the situation. It is restless and only hears its voice. It's full of arrogance and personal preferences. The brain has its preferences and dislikes, which it cherishes and will never abandon. Our minds can be the source of our demise. It could also be the catalyst for change and reaching our full potential.

Our brain is an unseen organ that generates ideas. It stores memories and feelings. Thoughts are just that: Thoughts. Our likes and dislikes are influenced by our past karma as well as our current karma. This changes the nature of the thoughts, making them either good or bad or even unbearable. Some thoughts make us happy. They have positive associations, whereas others make us sad because they hurt or hurt our ego. When we hold on firmly to our experiences or needs and wants, we start suffocating and seek support to live. Most of us probably have spent our entire lives feeling choked by our memories and thoughts, unable to inhale and live in freedom.

Our mind has the potential to be our best friend. It can assist us in focusing and concentrating on our tasks. It can assist us in defining and prioritising our life goals. Clarity of thought allows us to appreciate our lives, our work, the gifts we have been given, the various connections we have and the importance they help to shape us. A clear and calm mind reflects Divinity beautifully. The light of Creator within us shines as seen by all when our mind is pure.

When we learn how to overcome our dislikes and hatred, we can clean our minds. We must ruthlessly purge our minds of the evilness and rejections that lead to so many negative thoughts. We will stop being hurt and hurting others while we learn to be self-sufficient of our personal preferences and rely solely on Divinity. We will no longer be grumpy and will instead be joyful and balanced at all times. We must begin to recognize and let go of our inner ugliness.

Our mind enjoys directing and controlling others' actions. We will never be relaxed or peaceful as long as we play games of attempting to control others. We must recognise the right of everyone to live out their lives as they wish and accept and spend our lives as we desire. We must be aware of our goals in life and work hard to achieve them. We must not rely on others to assist us in achieving our goals. Others begin manipulating us as soon as they realise we are reliant on them. And everyone suffers as a result of this. Our minds require constant love and admiration.

XXIII

YOU ARE RESPONSIBLE FOR YOUR HAPPINESS.

You may just have observed yourself relying on others to make you happy on several occasions. They do it occasionally, but not all of the time.

Who can blame them, after all? None of us can blame them, even if we are irritated with them for not living up to our expectations of making us happy.

Many people are unaware that our well-being is entirely within our control. Nobody was put on this planet to make other people happy. This is not our or their job to make anyone happy, no matter how much we want to make other people happy and demand that they do the same for us. That is the harsh reality to which we must endure and awaken. No one will ever be able to make us unhappy once we realise that our happiness is our responsibility.

We have frequently entrusted the task of making ourselves happy to the world. Happiness becomes a thing of the past in this cruel world in which we live. We exist in a world in which makes you smile, giggle, or be happy is always rewarded, and the reward always seems to be costly. You'll put your trust in them, believing they're sincere, only to have them rip your soul out in the end.

Roy Bennett put it the best way he could. I've always expected others to make me happy, but I've always been let down. I was never happy until I took affairs into my own hands. You will live a happy and satisfying life if you learn to take responsibility for your happiness. You are the only one who knows how to make you happy. You always can try and keep yourself happy now that you've realised how no one owes you happiness. It's easy because happiness already exists within you; all you have to do now is bring it to light.

First and foremost, always remember that you are your source of joy, regardless of the situation or who is around you. Learn to be happy with yourself, your belongings, and who you are. This is critical because you will realise that you are self-sufficient and complete.

Make a conscious effort to be happy at all times. We can all control how we react to our emotions, something which many people are unaware of. When you are sad, you can choose to make yourself happy, and it will work. To be sure I'm not lying, think about how many times you've smiled and decided to act friendly with somebody you don't like because you had no choice?

One of the best parts about being in charge of your happiness is that no one could ever take away your grief. This is because you, not they, are the source of happiness.

This protects you from the emotional stability that others may exert over you, whether intentionally or unintentionally. We have complete ownership of our happiness because it is our responsibility. This is emotional liberty, and as I've said before when your happiness is in the palms of others, you're in an emotional prison, even if you don't realise it.

Today, set yourself free and take charge of your happiness. You would be emotionally independent and see the beauty in life.

XXIV

TIME DOES HEAL. GIVE TIME, SOME TIME

We rarely get through a period of grief, loss, or disappointment without hearing the adage "time heals all wounds" or "just give it some time," and it isn't always appreciated. Whether or not intent is there, when the grief is raw, the phrases almost sound cruel and insensitive. We can sometimes hear the words spoken to us in our voices. Nonetheless, there are times in life when we believe our broken hearts would never heal. We are supposed to believe that our suffering will go away despite our hopelessness and despair. Why does everyone keep repeating this phrase?

Take a look at the word in context. Words frequently lose their value as they travel through time, language, and culture. Perhaps the phrase has a deeper meaning. Although not everyone experiences the same amount or type of despair, the majority of people do so at some point in their lives. Humanity as a whole has a certain amount of common experience.

Perhaps that can provide some comfort – the knowledge that we are not the only ones suffering. We used to rely solely on each other to get us through difficult times.

Whether we should be healing physically or mentally, timing is crucial. We're more sensitive, irritable, and prone to infection. Even if we know better, we may tend to pick at open wounds. We must make an effort not to pick at ourselves caused by emotional healing, or we will not be able to heal properly. While we are in this sensitive state of mind, recapping tragic events or discovering "What-If" situations can be especially harmful. Throughout the healing process, we must remember to look after ourselves.

Our wounds leave scars no matter what happens and how well we heal. Emotional scars can sometimes be unsightly. We may be led down unidentified paths in our search for the truth, which can sometimes be very dangerous. We must ask the questions that lead us to the most effective solutions. We could think about just how time affects our grief. We recognise how our perspective might shift. We understand that simply believing something does not make it so. Faith allows us to consider the potential that something is true. New perspectives bring healing, but they take time to develop. There is just no simple explanation for this.

So, here it is again: Time does heal. Give time, some time.

XXV

FORGIVE BUT NEVER FORGET.

Forgiveness is simply a useful concept that has made religious organisations a lot of money over the centuries. You'd be surprised at just how much people would do to be forgiven of their guilt rather than fix the issues they caused.

Because it is never actually their fault, to begin with, we must always forgive everyone. Worse yet, the alternative involves you heating up over with rage (thus destroying your own life) and doing nothing. No amount of suffering you inflict on another can ever make up for the wrongs you've done. Kind acts, on the other hand, may startle them enough just to melt their hard hearts a little and save others from the same fate.

It's not a good idea to forget, because your memories are a big part of who you are. We would make the same mistakes every day, live miserable lives, and destroy the lives of everybody much more than a simple mistake we never made before if we chose to forget everything bad that ever happened.

Differentiating between unnecessarily wanting to improve things and working to do just that over time (which makes you feel better) and then letting go when you've done everything you can is the key.

Find new passions, new places, and new enlightenment paths where you can truly break free from the shackles of your hesitations, fears, regrets, and deceptions. We reach this eternal goal by living better lives and learning to treat others nicer as we feel more inclined to do so in our decent lives.

Don't stand for injustice, but don't hold grudges either. Act to put things right, then step back and let the rest happen. We can only control our actions from now on, not in the past, so dwelling on it is a waste of time and a ruin of the present. Take a step back and observe your sentiments from the outside. As if you were dealing with a child, be patient and keep reminding yourself that you don't need to give it a second thought.

Consider why you're having trouble doing something like this after a few weeks and what steps you can take to help your situation. Because the mind does not act irrationally, we must start paying attention and gain a different perspective when something does not appear to be right. Through mutual self-reflection, that is how we heal.

XXVI
SMILE AT A STRANGER.

"I'll never understand all the good that a simple smile can accomplish."

- Mother Teresa

The simple act of smiling at a stranger is a joyous gift. Even though it requires some thought and effort, recognising a person's humanity is free, takes very little time, and may just change the course of their day. I can't think of a better reason why I shouldn't smile at everyone when the opportunity arises. For a variety of reasons unknown to us, some people walk around feeling completely defeated. You don't need to know their tale; all you have to do is remind them that happiness still exists and that the world is larger than one's perception. Maybe you can turn someone's bad day into a good one!

Strive for "real" or genuine smiles rather than forced ones. The appearance and feel of one versus the other differ significantly, and most people have no trouble distinguishing the two.

Nothing is more irritating than being given a "fake" smile! To smile sincere, you must genuinely want to smile! When you're flashing that warm smile, think of something positive.

How often do you smile at someone else without considering whether or not they respond? Not everyone will return your smile, but most people will respond when you send a cosy sincere smile their way.

Don't take it personally if someone doesn't smile back at you. It doesn't necessarily mean you didn't warm their heart. Keep in mind that you never know exactly what is going on in someone's life at any given time if they do not acknowledge your smile in some way. That person could be having a bad day due to circumstances beyond your comprehension or something tragic happening in their life; your smile might be the only bright spot in their day.

Smiling at people can help them feel accepted, encourage them to be positive, and even give them a sense of self-worth. When their world seems to be crumbling around them, your smile may be the ray of hope that all is not lost.

XXVII

BE A GOOD LISTENER.

" Everyone has a story to tell, all they need is someone to listen."

- Siddhant Sharma

Whenever it comes to your listening abilities, how would you rate yourself?

There are a set of abilities that are useful in any conversation, whether it's about sports, mental wellbeing, or anything in between. It's important to establish a foundation of listening skills, irrespective of how light or heavy the topic is.

Find an opportunity to have a conversation.

Make a welcoming environment and provide an opportunity for a conversation. The first step in having a meaningful conversation with someone else is to create the opportunity for you to do so in a place where you are both comfortable. Offer someone an opportunity to talk if you believe they are in need and attempt to open up. Invite them to join you for a drink. Offer to grab a bite to eat. By offering, you've made yourself easily accessible to listen if they want to talk, and by deciding on a relaxing setting, the conversation will be less pressured and stressful.

Speak Less, Listen More

Staying available in a conversation is difficult for many of us, but we may not realise it. One of the most common challenges with being available is that people are constantly thinking about what they should say next. You'll pay attention to the first few minutes of what the person is saying, then your mind will be preoccupied with what you need to say once they're finished. Or they may share a personal issue with you, and you immediately try to come up with a solution. This isn't going to happen. This isn't the same as listening.

Silence is pleasant too.

Silence can be uncomfortable, but it doesn't have to be. We sometimes try to fill the void left by silence by talking, but this only serves to keep the conversation from moving any further or more meaningful way.

People can think and gain actual insight about what's being discussed when there are silences. It allows us to process new information and consider how it affects us. It also allows us to think about what to speak next and what questions to ask. It gives us the ability to feel and be exposed.

Don't be afraid to ask questions.

Ensure you're asking questions that help you realise what the person is saying when you're listening to them share something difficult. When a person knows they've been listened to, it's one of the most important aspects of feeling validated.

By asking a question and mirroring what they've said, you're demonstrating that you're paying attention and trying to understand. "So here is what I heard, so this is what you meant?" for example alternatively "So this is what you're saying. Do I understand correctly?" It is a simple question that demonstrates that you've been paying attention and, more importantly, that you've taken steps to ensure that you understand what they've said.

There's nothing as the right thing to say.

We mistakenly assume that the one tough discussion will be the last. We believe we only have one chance to make the other person's conversation meaningful. That is simply not the case. Stressing over how you'll say all of it perfectly will take you out of the moment to make you a poor listener. Be aware of what's going on around you, pay attention to what's being said, and honestly take part in the conversation.

You don't want to be the conversation's hero. Being heard and accepted is more valuable to the other person than any suggestions you could give. You can always talk about it later.

XXVIII

CHANGE IS INEVITABLE. BE READY FOR IT.

"Some people come in your life as blessings. Others come in your life as lessons"

- Mother Teresa

Many people adopted this old saying and drove with it. It took some time for this saying to sink in for some people, including myself. I had to learn it the hard way. People are temporary. Life does not come to an end until your heart stops beating, but till then, things continue to move forward and change.

People change and advance in the same way that life does. We've advanced from babies to toddlers, children and teens, and finally adults. We've had a lot of friends over the years. We've known them since we were kids, and some of them have been with us since the beginning. We have seen it all, from birthday parties to sleepovers. We started to notice a difference. We began to notice a shift. We have no idea when it first began to appear, or even when we first became aware of it. Everything was great when we started high school, and now that we've graduated and moved on to college, we've found our areas of interest. We've noticed that the gap is widening.

We don't like some things anymore, and we don't get along as well as we used to. It is often the most painful thing seeing someone you used to know all about turn into a stranger with a few memories. As I made progress through college, I had far too many cases of this. Friends I'd known for years started to change and end up leaving one by one. It was as if I were merely a pit stop, and now that they'd been refreshed, it was time for them to move on.

People who chose to leave my life taught me a valuable lesson. People who have shaped me into the person I am today. We all had different passions, dreams, and goals, as well as various perspectives to achieving them. It wasn't them, and it wasn't me who had done it. It was just a part of life. Everyone you meet has a purpose. Whether it's to teach you things about yourself or life before they leave or to bless you and walk alongside you for the rest of your life, they're there. It's never just a coincidence when something happens.

Some of my friends have stayed and others have gone away. Life keeps changing. I wish I could say I've fully accepted it, but I've come a long way in terms of accepting it. It's okay to be disappointed about it at times; however, don't dwell on it. Life goes on, and you should, too.

XXIX

YOU CAN'T PLEASE EVERYONE.

"You can't please everyone, because everyone can't please you".

-*Siddhant Sharma*

While humanity may have begun from a specific source, the fact remains that we are all diverse. We all have different lives, beliefs, values, relationships, thoughts, and feelings. On a variety of levels, we raise our kids differently, think differently, and behave differently.

Even though we share common traits, we are all unique individuals. And, because we are all different, with differing views and working methods, we often mistakenly believe that our way is the best way to go about things. It's easy to see why we're critical of others as a result of this. That may also explain why it is impossible in life to please everyone. That could be one of the reasons why people are unhappy with our decisions. That could be why, no matter what you do, think, or feel, someone will be surprised or dissatisfied by the mere thought of your choices, or even your existence. How can they possibly believe, say, or act the way they do?

It's impossible to please everyone. It's simply impossible. Someone will disapprove of everything you do, from how you say things to your child to what outfit you wear, what you do for a living, where and what you eat, how you drive your car, how you pay your bills, and everything in between. You must not try to please people all of the time. It simply isn't worth it. You'll not only start living your life according to someone's standards, but you'll also lose any sense of joy or enthusiasm. Just do what makes you feel good and pleases you. All that matters is that you're doing the right thing with a good heart.

When you know people have been talking behind your back, or in front of your face, it's difficult to stay on track. People enjoy saying hurtful things to others. It helps to boost their egos and enable their outspoken personalities for various reasons. There are many reasons why it is impossible to satisfy everybody, whereas this information may not completely lessen your concerns, clear your mind, or eliminate all of your fears about following your dreams, it should help you realise that no one will always be completely satisfied with your actions.

What matters is that you do what you want. Don't worry about what other people think you should be doing. Allowing that to influence the path of your dreams and hopes is not a good idea. When it's something you're extremely passionate about and have always wished to do in your life, don't let that hinder your spirit or cause you to change your course.

Don't ever surrender to your dreams and hopes because you're trying to make people happy. Our family's happiness is important to us to some extent. Our friends' joy is also infectious. But not to the point where we begin to give up everything we've ever desired and wished for in life.

Allowing peer pressure to slow you down is a bad idea. Set your sights on the stars. Anything is possible if you are focused enough. It makes no difference what other people think or say about you. What matters is that you're doing something that makes you happy. You must never feel sorry for yourself as long as you're satisfied deep down inside and just doing things for the right reasons with the right motivations.

XXX

TO KNOW FEAR IS THE END OF IT.

Consider your most important goal. Why haven't you finished it already? If you think like most of them the answer is simple: Fear. Fear is the major hurdle that prevents you from achieving your goals. Fear can cause us to become distracted and make excuses, but it doesn't have to. One of the most liberating efforts you can undertake is learning to overcome fear.

It's easy to deny that fear is affecting you and to give excuses for not achieving what you're capable of. Treat fear as a command to action, not an excuse, rather than turning around and trying to hide from it. Take a look at your objective. If you let fear keep you from achieving your goal, you've effectively given up. This is why, to overcome fear, you must first realise the fears and false beliefs that are holding you back.

If you don't understand the mechanisms of fear, learning how to overcome it can be a daunting task. Recognize that fear is a natural evolutionary response before you chastise yourself for feeling afraid. Your brain and heart are trying to communicate with you, even if it doesn't feel like it right now. You can forever overcome fear if you learn to read the signals.

Understanding how to overcome the fear is similar to learning how to solve any other problem in that you must first identify the problem. What exactly are you afraid of? Take a few minutes to sit quietly and monitor your thoughts, feelings, and bodily sensations. Make a list of all that comes to mind, and be as precise as possible. Consider starting daily mindfulness-based practice to gain a better understanding of your real motives. You'll feel empowered to face your fears once you've found your centre.

There are times when you should act and times when you should reflect. When you act too quickly to conquer your fear, you may lead to more problems than good, such as trying to reach for a drink, enjoying a delicious meal, or even suppressing the emotion entirely. Try something new the next time you're afraid: do nothing. Take a few minutes to sit with your fear. Consider it for a moment. What is the cause of the issue? What is your storey about why you are unable to overcome this fear? This is not to say that you should not act. A few moments of reflection can help you overcome fear in a productive, deliberate, and effective manner.

When you're scared, you tend to isolate yourself. What happens if you start making a blunder? What if you don't succeed? You begin to believe that you can't make any progress, that you're incapable of doing so – fear brings you down. Adopting a growth mindset is one of the most effective ways to overcome fear and anxiety. It's not about reaching your goal and being flawless at all times. Stop striving for perfection since no one is ever flawless all of the time. The framework of a growth mindset is becoming satisfied with what you don't know and continuing regardless.

Everyone fails at some point. Top business owners. Leaders of the world. Chefs of note. Artists, scientists, and doctors, to name a few. Our society avoids discussing failure in favour of celebrating successes, giving the wrong illusion that to be successful, one must never fail. Accept that everybody on the planet, even those you know and admire, has failed on their way to greatness as a part of overcoming fear. The sooner you realise that your fear of failure is keeping you from pursuing your goals, the sooner you'll be able to accept the chance of failure and move on.

What differs you from the rest of the group is how you handle fear. To know fear will help you learn to conquer it.

XXXI

PERSPECTIVE DOES MATTER.

In the ocean, a small wave was having a great time bobbing around. He was enjoying the breeze and the cool air until he realised the other waves crashing against the shore in front of him.

"My God, this is terrible," the wave said. Take a look at what's about to happen to me!"

Then there was the third wave. "Why do you look sad?" it asked the first wave, who was looking depressed.

"You don't understand!" said the first wave. We're all going to have a crash!

"No, you don't understand," the second wave said. You're not a wave, but a part of the huge ocean.

The way you see things has a clear link with how you feel.

If you can figure out what's driving the other person's perspective, you might be successful in convincing them to change their opinion (or your own). It's essential to understand what inspires people's actions, whether you're trying to get your child to eat vegetables or try and convince a signing off on a large purchase. Understanding the motivations behind other people's decisions will give you the tools you need to sway them in your favour. Understanding your opponent's different points of view will save you a lot of disappointment and even anger.

Why is it essential to take a different approach to things? You can get two ideas from this:

If another person is confident about something you don't understand, there's a reason for it. You don't need to make your point. To bridge the gap, you must first understand their point of view.

Is it even relevant? Just let it go in, everyday matters.

Detaching yourself from your point of view will provide you with the perspective you lack when holding tight to your position and trying to convince the other side.

Take a step back and observe the situation as if you were a bystander.

You will be better positioned to offer solutions that meet their needs if you could see the desire behind the other side's arguments. You may not have to comply with their viewpoint; you may believe their position is incorrect or foolish, or both; however, until you understand, you will be unable to find a solution.

You don't understand how others' logic works if you judge them as stupid or wrong. Their differing perspectives are usually derived from a set of facts via some form of reasoning. Recognizing that reasoning may enable you to point out where the facts are incorrect or incomplete, as well as where the reasoning is flawed. Get a grip on the situation and try to figure out why people respond the way they do. Become a keeper of different perspectives rather than becoming disappointed, irritated, or angry. You'll expand your intellectual horizons, become more emphatic, and feel less stressed, hurt, or disappointed.

Our viewpoints shift more frequently than we believe is possible. I'm glad I'm no longer the person I was 8 years ago. Some of my viewpoints have become stronger and clarified. Others don't exist.

XXXII

MAKE EVERY MOMENT MEMORABLE.

People's minds are usually obsessed with a variety of things, making it difficult to enjoy the present moment.

It is a common blunder for people to fail to enjoy every moment of their lives. Numerous factors influence this mindset, due to the busy world we live in. Work, family responsibilities, careers, challenges, and a variety of other factors all play a role.

People tend to think ahead and be concerned more about tomorrow, ignoring that each passing moment is important to live and that there is no way to undo the mistakes of the past.

Fortunately, you can turn your day around and make it meaningful. A purposeful and meaningful life is a rare thing. Here are some ways how I do it.

Smile.

As I have mentioned before, Perspective is everything.

The most important aspect of living a happy life is how you perceive things and how you understand situations. It takes a lot of effort and practice to be an optimist. Without a doubt, there are some situations in your life over which you have no control and over which your emotions have complete control. But even so, there are many other ways to fight negative thoughts, the most important of which is learning to pause. Everything else that is happening to you and around you should be put on hold. If someone has said something negative about you, take a moment to consider it. If your feelings are on the verge of exploding, take a breath and then make a decision.

Second, remember to smile. A smile improves your mood and impacts your way of thinking. As a result, smiling is extremely contagious.

Love what you do.

Most people seem to hate their jobs and careers daily. There might be times when you wished to quit your job due to insulting bosses or undesirable workplace events.

Putting your motivation on your table, or maybe on digital screens, is one way to get rid of this type of thinking. It might be a photo of your family or a note to motivate yourself. It assists you in becoming more motivated and dedicated to your work.

Try new things.

Remember the last time you experimented with new things? Always ask that question to yourself as it will help you come up with new challenges and ways to make your days more meaningful and enjoyable.

If you are afraid of such things, it may be beneficial to step outside of your comfort bubble.

Focus on what's important.

Focusing on what's important in your life, depending on your vision and goals, can help you assess what is currently on your plate.

It also ensures that you know which paths you are ready to take. As a result, it leaves out the things that are both a burden and a waste of time.

Don't forget to laugh.

" Laughter is the best medicine " – as simple as it may sound, it truly does heal a wide range of negative emotions. Having a good time counts as well. With this mindset, you will be able to recall your days more brightly and enjoy every moment of your life.

Living beyond imperfection, in the end, always will make your life meaningful.

XXXIII

NEVER TAKE THINGS FOR GRANTED.

Unfortunately, we all tend to exaggerate and describe every event and engagement that occurs in our daily lives that appears to go wrong.

My statement for this discussion is that we all need to take a step back from time to time, take some deep breaths, and reflect on the abundance we already have in our lives before searching for more things to buy to be happy.

How about our senses, well-being, jobs, and relationships, in addition to the materialistic things we take for granted? We all expect our sight, hearing, smell, taste, and touch to be flawless when we're young. These senses, however, may not be as strong as they once were as we get older. You'll likely take these senses for granted until you lose your sight or your hearing ability. This applies to any health issues that arise as a result of ageing or accidents, and we should always be grateful when everything in our bodies is working properly. Never take for granted your good health. Protect and nurture your health as if it were the jewels of your life.

Let us talk about our jobs now. How many people do you know who genuinely enjoy their work? Everyone is constantly discussing the negative aspects of their jobs. Complaining about how they don't earn enough, that they work too long hours, that they don't get enough vacation time, that their bosses are insensitive, or that they can't stand their coworkers. One day they lose their job, and without a place to work, everything they used to make a fuss about no longer seems so bad. Yet, while they did work there, they took for granted what they had rather than working to improve their situation daily.

Finally, who doesn't have a problem with their families, spouses, children, or in-laws? It's easier to focus on the flaws in these relationships rather than the positive aspects. People usually take their connections for granted until they die, divorce, or become estranged from them. This is unfortunate because true happiness should come from appreciating and cherishing everything mentioned above – every day as we have it. Don't put a high value on something you once had until you've lost it. It's impossible to return in time and regain what you thought you had.

XXXIV

PARENTS ARE AS IMPORTANT AS CHILDREN, DON'T COMPARE.

"Don't take things for granted," is perhaps the best piece of advice that has stood the test of time. Particularly your parents!

I must state that I am not speaking for anyone who has had a difficult time communicating with their parents as a child or as an adult. As I grew up, I noticed many young people say hurtful things about their parents. Similarly, I've known parents who have made insulting comments about their children. Each of those stories, I'm sure, has two sides. I also know a lot of adults who have broken up with their parents. That being said, we'll be dealing with the world's positive, nurturing, and caring parents, who, I'm assuming, account for the vast majority of parents.

I've always considered myself lucky to have parents who genuinely cared about me and always put my needs ahead of their own. My parents were bound to make daily sacrifices to keep us safe, secure, healthy, and happy. Their wants and needs were always put on hold so that they could afford the best for us. And the term "afford" did not refer to debit card limits or cash advances back then; rather, it referred to how much money they were able to save – a few thousand dollars – by working long and hard hours.

My parents are good people who lived in the city and knew how to save money better than anyone I'd ever met. Neither of them was a driver. They never had a debit card, and my mother waited until she was in her forties to open a joint account with me. Dad set a fine example by paying his bills the day after they arrived in his bank account. My parents would probably get a 10/10 for their ability to pay their bills well before they were due for the rest of their lives.

Great parents always show up to be there for you whenever you need them. It is not necessary to beg them to assist you in a time of need. They want to make sure, however, that they are not a permanent crutch that prevents you from walking on your own. Great parents know how to allow their children to mature, become self-sufficient, and share their love with others. Simply love and respect them, and their world will always be yours.

I could go on for a few more chapters describing my parents, whom I consider fantastic. But, at this point, I'd like to return to the first paragraph's premise. And that's why you should never underestimate the importance of your parents. "Your parents will not be there forever," is a lesson to learn and remember.

With that in mind, I recommend that you do everything possible to make your parents happy and proud. Always treat them with the respect that they have earned. Great parents never expect anything in return for their years of sacrifice and good deeds from their children. They only care about their children being healthy, happy, and secure while leading decent and respectable lives. Remind them frequently that you are fine, and shower them with hugs and kind words that will brighten their day. Parents are Special. Remind your parents how important they are to you regularly.

XXXV
CHOOSE YOUR FRIENDS WISELY.

The term "friend" can be defined in a variety of ways. They can be anything from "someone with whom you want to spend your valuable time" to "someone for the one you would drop it all and fly to a different nation to get them out of trouble." These are two completely different viewpoints of the same word. The second definition is for someone who has earned your trust and respect. This lesson is aimed toward people between the ages of 13 to 30, because I believe that this is the time in life when people are most impacted by their "as such friends."

If you've ever been the parent of a teenager, you realise how much social influence can impact your child's life. Recognition by peers appears to be extremely important to teenagers. In many tragic cases, the desire to be accepted outshines parental advice and the use of common sense. For instance, if teens are pressured by their "peers" that smoking cigarettes and drinking beer is necessary to fit in, it may be tough for them to resist. They have no idea that the decisions they make at this young age will have a significant impact on their future lifestyle habits and well-being.

As a result, I believe it is critical to "Select Your Friends Wisely" at this stage and throughout life. Ignoring relationships with those who insist on indulging is the only way to avoid creating bad habits such as drinking and smoking as a teen. Even though this may be easier said than done, we all know it is possible. Teenage boys and girls mature fast and become college kids. Even those who avoided unhealthy habits in school will be put to the test in college, far from home.

Even if students have chosen level-minded friends to associate with within school and college, their place of work will become the next stop on their mission to make good decisions. Going out for a few beers with coworkers after work one night can easily turn into going out for beers up to four nights a week. The explanation for doing so can be traced back to job stress and a desire to take a break and drink after work. Associating with people who drink too much has the disadvantage of making you dependent on alcohol. Even if these people choose to stay at home at night, they may buy a six-pack and watch TV to loosen up at home.

The importance of choosing those you relate with wisely becomes clear in the above scenario. Relationships always start innocently enough, but if you socialize with people who overindulge in anything, you should stay away from them at all costs. Individuals who are unaware of what is happening to them are more likely to develop bad habits. Family and friends are often the first to notice a person's changes in behaviour.

Friendships and associates have chosen wisely can lead to a life of safety and wealth. If happiness and peace of mind are important to you, choose your friends carefully.

XXXVI

WHAT YOU DO TODAY WILL DETERMINE WHO YOU WILL BE TOMORROW.

Between where you are now and where you will be tomorrow, there is a thin line. That one small habit you rehearse every day is the line that connects the two. You will break down slowly and gradually, day by day if you lean into unhealthy habits (or ignore the good ones), but if you practise healthy habits, you will set yourself up gradually over time, day by day.

I completely neglected myself during the first three months of writing this book. I stopped exercising, socialising, and exercising, and I stopped taking care of myself. What's the result? I was miserable, with sleepless nights, constant tension and worry, emotional stress, and confusion.

Luckily, as soon as I realised I was engaging in self-destructive behaviour, I made a vow that I would never allow myself to sink to this level again. Since then, I've developed some daily habits that I continue to follow to this day. They include daily morning meditation for 15 minutes, journal writing, daily stretching and workout, and intermittent fasting.

Every day, we are exposed to new challenges, some of which are larger and more serious than others. We must look inwards and ignite the strength and courage that permits us to pick ourselves up and carry on, regardless of the emotional wreckage we may find ourselves in. How are we going to accomplish this? We rely on our daily habits to keep us going. Our lifestyle routines and self-care rituals shape the rhythm of our lives and the direction in which they progress because what you do today will determine who you will be tomorrow.

Do you want to know where you'll be a year from now? Take a look at what you're doing right now. Do you want to be a musician someday? Are you trying to practice today? Do you desire to be in the best physical condition of your life? That's fantastic, but did you work out today? Because you become, what you do today.

Do your best to stick with whatever those day-to-day anchors, practises, and rituals are because breakthroughs don't occur overnight breakthroughs happen when small changes in your daily life compound into something fabulous over time.

XXXVII
BELIEVE IN YOURSELF.

" Believing in yourself is the first step of being unstoppable"

-Siddhant Sharma

Let's be clear about something: Nothing will change in your life unless you take any steps to create the change you desire. And, to be honest, if you don't trust in your potential to bring about such a change in the first place, you're getting nowhere. Part of this is because your brain is wired to keep you in your comfort zone, but the other factor is that you don't believe in yourself, so you don't bother to go after what you want.

Because every move you make—or avoid—is based on a set of belief systems, the first step is to change the belief system, not to build confidence and to take action. Analyze yourself from the inside out, do a reality check, and rewrite the script of the storey you tell yourself over and over:

I am confident in my ability to solve problems as they pop up. I'm confident that I'll be able to weather when it arrives.

When the wind blows, I know I can adjust my sails. When the obstacles pile up, I'm confident that I'll be able to find a way around them. I believe I am capable of accomplishing what I have set out to do.

The light that ignites your confidence is self-belief. And it's your self-confidence that motivates you to try new things that take you out of your comfort zone.

It's not about boasting about what you've achieved or speaking about what you're going to do to achieve self-confidence. No. The path to true self-confidence is to do the polar opposite: Talk less and let your actions speak. Why? Because real confidence is expressed through actions that go unnoticed.

XXXVIII

KEEP AN OPEN MIND.

"Don't be too timid and squeamish about your actions. All life is an experiment."

- Ralph Waldo Emerson

People who don't realise this, I believe, are those who don't have fun in life—they forget to play, and as a result, they lose contact with their inner artistic child. They're the ones who avoid taking action and making changes. They're the ones who regret not having had the boldness to live the life that was authentic to themselves.

People who understand that life is an experiment have more fun than any other. They put things to the test. They are the ones who break things. They realise opportunities and act on them. They do what makes them feel alive, and they put themselves into their work. Above all, they dare to follow their hearts, fully aware that they will make mistakes along the way, which is fine because it is through mistakes that they will learn.

Fortunately, I've chosen the latter mindset because I believe life is an experiment—and I want that to be the largest, brightest, most awesome and artistic, wild, fun, and thrilling experiment I've ever lived so in ten years I can look back and say, "I'm glad I did."

As a creative, I'm beginning to see that excellence in any field is a combination of art and science. You must express your character, enthusiasm, and authenticity in the art section. You must explore the process, gain some experience, develop your skills, and develop strategies from the science part.

So here's what I'd say to you: Maintain an open imagination and act as if you're an artist, but imagine, fail, and learn as if you're a scientist. To put it another way, be yourself and make silly mistakes, but don't repeat them.

When you understand that life is merely an experiment, you will stop kneeling to fear and greatly lower your risk of living a life of regret. You'll begin to do things that bring you back to life. In other words, you begin to tell a better story, and who doesn't enjoy a good story?

XXXIX

DON'T REGRET IT.

While we're all sitting around getting depressed for doing what we've done, it only tends to prove the belief that this is how things will always be in the future. Our thoughts programme our brains, and if we keep on thinking that negative stuff will happen in the future, we are setting ourselves up to fail. The trick is to let go of our mistakes because we will all experience failures at some point in our lives. Because all we're doing, in my opinion, is learning.

If you don't understand what I'm saying, I advise that you think about what you expect from life. To get to the right place, you often have to be wrong. Make more of an effort to notice the things from which you should be learning. If we expect to be disappointed all of the time, life will always find a way to show us that. We are all flawed, and we all make errors to learn from our mistakes.

You will never realise that holding that red hot chunk of hate in your heart is letting you look into yourself and the decisions you make if you keep it there. It allows you to take a different direction in life. It is entirely up to you what you do with your choices. There is something to be learned from each failure, and life will continue to try to teach you, and those circumstances will continue to occur until you make an actual change. Wouldn't it be wonderful if you suddenly realised you'd made the right choice on this one? You are the mastermind behind your fate. Keep that in mind.

Another reason not to take your previous decisions to the heart is how it allows you to think low of yourself. When something bad happens to us, we all torture ourselves mentally. "Why am I so stupid?". And statements like "I'm such an idiot"! To get the most out of any situation, you must get rid of your mental weakness. Be gentle with yourself and realise that this setback may be a stepping stone to your true calling. In ten years, you never know where you'll be. Don't hold back from being harsh with yourself. It was exactly what you always wanted at one point.

Your know-how, as humans, we all do what we want to do? Don't we usually give some thought to our words and actions? Then don't be too hard on yourself for evaluating your options, aiming for the stars, and then falling short. It happens to most of us. You aren't a child who is told what to do about his or her life. You are a complete and workable human being. And you know what's best for you, even if it occasionally goes badly!

All the things you must have could have, or would have done, no matter how often you think about it. It won't change the outcome.

The only person you're burdening with your suffering is yourself. It prevents you from living the life you want to live, and the visions you want to make a reality will continue to elude you. It's the equivalent of holding a hot lump of coal in your palms and hoping that it will burn somebody else. There's no reason why that pain should continue to bother you. Stop reliving it in your mind. Make a point of doing good things and help you to develop as a person. Make yourself as valuable as possible. You are so deserving of it. You can let go of it and allow the experience to mould you into the person you've always wished to be.

Never look back on a single day of your life; good days bring happiness, bad days bring experiences, the worst days bring lessons, and the best days bring memories.

So keep in mind that no day is wasted.

XL

LOVE UNCONDITIONALLY.

" She was a simple, homely young lady from a small town with many ambitions. He was a simple individual with a good career. They met by chance, she fell in love, and he recognised his emotions for her as well. She regarded him as her entire world. He knew her better than anyone else. He wanted to make sure she had everything she needed. She wanted to make him happy in any way she could.

He wished for her to rise from the limits of her home and become self-sufficient. He wanted her to learn to deal with society's harsh realities and establish a career so that she could survive if something happened to him in the future. He was always advising her and punishing her when she made errors. He was shaping her for the wellbeing of herself. She was having a lot of success, and a lot of men were interested in her. Oh, and did I say she was beautiful? She had a heart-warming smile that filled anyone's, heart.

She grew more confident as time went on, and her profession was reaching its pinnacle. But he has always been there for her, guiding her and pushing her to make more progress. She, on the other hand, was no longer fond of him offering her advice. She believed she was more than capable of making her own decisions. He, too, was always working, and the gap between them began to widen. She had no idea why he was always pressuring her to do more and more. But she began to argue with him.

He was upset. He couldn't understand why she started to feel bad about him, even though he had cherished her since she was a simple, homely girl. How can she say such things to a man who has always wanted her to be self-sufficient, who has been proud of her every time she reaches a new level of success? He left her with the words:"

"Perhaps your ego has grown so large as a result of your success that you are unable to feel my sentiments for you in your heart." I loved you. My goal was to make you feel better, and not bad. Perhaps it was my failure that, after all of our time together, I couldn't get you to understand who you are to me and what I wanted for you. I only wanted the best for you, and I hoped you would be more successful than I was. I hope you don't make the same errors that I did. May you find everything you've ever wished."

Unconditional love is a big word for something most people don't get.

The term "unconditional love" does not indicate "love without boundaries." It's to love without expecting anything in return.

The above means that when we give our love, we do so without expecting anything in return. In our relationships, it's critical to show this kind of unconditional love. Otherwise, we are providing love with "strings attached". Power and influence imbalances consequence as a result of this. Understanding to rely on the stress of those obstacles by offering connection, love, and understanding, as well as accepting implication, creating compromises, and progressing forward in a way that benefits both parties is one of life's most beautiful experiences.

Compassion, respect, and safety are all basic expectations in our relationships. If these aren't met, we may have to impose clear restrictions. Trying to distance oneself or cutting oneself off entirely are examples of these boundaries. If you do cut off, it's doesn't indicate that you have made a conditional offer of love. Remember that they are not bound to you because of your love. They are not obligated to you in any way. However, you owe it to yourself to be safe, respectful, and kind. You can walk away from people you care deeply about to take care of your safety and needs.

A Final Word.

It's all about achieving peace in life. The goal of life is to reach the peak of happiness. If we are lonely, life appears scary, which is why we develop relationships.

We don't want to want to be alone, and we may not want to try new things. We are all living in pristine conditions.

The goal of life is to achieve liberation from the cycle of reincarnation.

Keep Living!

www.ingramcontent.com/pod-product-compliance
Lightning Source LLC
Chambersburg PA
CBHW020733160726
47993CB00006B/2436